Vivian Steele: The Queen of Wall Street

Henrique M. Simões

Dedicated to all traders, who share both the toughest
and most stimulating profession in the world.

TABLE OF CONTENTS

INTRODUCTION

Vivian Steele is a highly skilled and stunning trader. Revered as the city's foremost trader, Vivian consistently surprises her peers with her sharp intellect and exceptional ability to generate profits. Her charm and playful flirting add an alluring touch to her persona, keeping everyone captivated.

Name: Vivian Steele

Occupation: Professional Trader

Background: Vivian Steele is a sophisticated and modern figure in the financial world, distinguished by her background in mathematics, finance, and her collaboration on various NASA projects. This unique blend equips her with a distinctive perspective in trading. Starting her finance career as a quantitative analyst, Vivian quickly recognized her adeptness at interpreting market data and forecasting short-term trends with remarkable precision.

Personality: Vivian possesses a razor-sharp intellect and an unyielding mindset. She approaches trading with a calculated, methodical approach, never allowing emotions to cloud her judgment. Her keen eye for detail enables her to sift effortlessly through vast amounts of data, identifying opportunities where others see chaos. Despite her intense focus and competitive nature, she maintains a cool, composed demeanor, exuding confidence in her abilities.

Skills and Abilities:

Analytical Genius: Vivian excels at dissecting complex market data and extracting valuable insights. She utilizes advanced statistical models and algorithms to discern patterns and trends, giving her a significant edge in the fast-paced world of trading.

Strategic Thinking: Vivian is a master strategist, always planning several steps ahead. She carefully assesses risks and rewards, crafting meticulous trading plans to maximize profits while minimizing potential losses.

Information Mastery: Vivian possesses an encyclopedic knowledge of financial markets, economic indicators, and geopolitical events. She stays current with breaking news and market developments, swiftly integrating new information into her trading strategies.

Mental Toughness: Vivian exhibits unwavering mental resilience, thriving under pressure and adapting swiftly to rapidly changing market conditions. She views setbacks as opportunities for growth and remains steadfast in her pursuit of success.

Intuition: In addition to relying on data and analysis, Vivian trusts her intuition when making trading decisions. She possesses a sixth sense for market movements, often sensing shifts in sentiment before they manifest in the data.

Appearance: Vivian cuts a striking figure with her sharp business attire and commanding presence. Tall and poised, she exudes an aura of confidence and authority, commanding respect from colleagues and competitors alike. Her striking good looks are matched by her preference for killer stilettos, completing her formidable image in any boardroom or trading floor.

Now it's time to meet her trading colleagues. Coming from diverse backgrounds and possessing varying trading abilities, her resident trader colleagues will add depth to the stories unfolding within those walls adorned with tickers and monitors.

Victor Fortune is an eccentric risk-taker in the stock market. He relies on superstitions and gut feelings to inform his trades, interpreting signs from various sources such as traffic lights, license plates, or even subliminal messages in dice games. Despite his unorthodox approach, Victor consistently achieves profitable outcomes, baffling others with his seemingly innate ability. His unconventional methods and flashy appearance further contribute to the intrigue surrounding his enigmatic persona.

John Spinner is a reckless trader and compulsive gambler, is driven by impulse and finds himself constantly at the mercy of his trades. He epitomizes the emotional and impulsive trader, often falling prey to enthusiasms that result in significant losses. With the finesse of a bull in a China shop, John charges through the market without restraint. Coupled with his rough appearance, uncouth manners, and unrefined language, he navigates the market with all the grace of a junkyard dog.

Meet **Mortimer Sagecroft**, a seasoned speculator known for his distinguished white hair and authoritative voice. Highly respected in his field, Mortimer is considered a veteran in speculation. However, despite his extensive knowledge, he struggles to mentor others due to his stern demeanor and the widespread ignorance among his trading colleagues. Mortimer doesn't say much, but when he does, it's with the weight of a lifetime of experience in financial markets. He's wary of newcomers looking for shortcuts. On the trading floor, Mortimer stands as a symbol of expertise, his wisdom shaped by years of market ups and downs.

Maxwell Dither is the epitome of chronic indecision in the trading world. Maxwell's talent lies not in making successful trades, but in annoying those around him with inventive excuses, envy, and excessive politeness. Despite spending all his time at the brokerage, rumors suggest he's never executed a single transaction. Maxwell is a living paradox—a character entrenched in the world of trading yet seemingly unable to commit to any action. His affliction with severe risk aversion only compounds his struggles, rendering him paralyzed by fear whenever an opportunity arises.

Bradley Downfall is known for his incurable condition: chronic pessimism that influences every aspect of his trading. He firmly believes, without any doubt, that the markets will inevitably decline, regardless of any evidence suggesting otherwise. Additionally, he wakes up in a bad mood and goes to bed feeling even worse, constantly angry with everyone and everything, including the markets.

Meet **Carter Data**, a trader known for his love of numbers and data-driven decision-making. Carter meticulously analyzes market trends and financial data to uncover opportunities and risks. He believes in making informed decisions based on empirical evidence. However, despite his dedication to analysis, Carter sometimes faces unexpected challenges in the unpredictable world of financial markets. He learns that while numbers are powerful tools, they don't always guarantee success. This contrast between his methodical approach and the market's unpredictability shapes Carter's journey as a trader.

Meet **Ryder Riskmore**, a fearless trader who thrives on taking risks in the financial world. Ryder never hesitates to dive into investments, embracing uncertainty and the unknown. His motto is "nothing ventured, nothing gained," reflecting his belief that greater risks lead to greater rewards. Ryder's investment strategy involves high-stakes maneuvers, prioritizing potential gains over caution. He disregards cautionary tales and conservative approaches, preferring the excitement of navigating unpredictable market currents. While some may see Ryder's approach as reckless, he views it as a calculated dance with risk, often resulting in favorable outcomes. Ryder Riskmore proves that in finance, taking risks can lead to the most rewarding outcomes.

THE ARRIVAL OF VIVIAN STEELE

John felt a mix of awe and intimidation as he watched a female trader enter the office. Her presence was commanding, exuding confidence with every step she took in form-fitting business attire and sleek black high heels that clicked seductively against the polished floor.

"Carter, who's that powerhouse?" John asked, his curiosity tinged with admiration.

Carter Data shook his head, a touch of uncertainty in his voice. *"No idea, never seen her around here. Must be from the SEC* or something... Scary stuff!"*

The woman approached them confidently. *"Good afternoon, gentlemen! My name is Vivian Steele. I've recently opened an account and look forward to trading alongside you."*

John gaped at her in astonishment, his mouth hanging open as he tried to process her commanding presence. *"Good afternoon... yes... here?!"* he stammered, clearly taken aback.

Carter contemplated for a moment, his smile widening with appreciation. *"Welcome! And good luck, of course!"*

Vivian wasted no time, immediately diving into action. She swiftly pulled documents out of her bag, grabbed a notebook, and rifled through her notes with impressive speed. Glancing at the ticker quotes displayed on the screens, she compared them with her meticulously organized notes, fully absorbed in her task.

John leaned over to Carter, whispering with a hint of amazement, *"I'm getting dizzy!"* They both chuckled nervously, feeling the palpable intensity Vivian brought to the room.

Without missing a beat, Vivian announced, *"Buy 2,000 Excel Energy (EXEN) at the market. I repeat, 2,000 Excel Energy (EXEN) at the market!"*

Just then, Bradley Downfall walked in, astonished by the commotion. *"Good morning! I just heard a buying order for Excel Energy (EXEN)... No energy stock is going to rise in this market context. The recession will reduce demand for energy resources and—"*

Vivian cut him off, her voice steady and almost robotic in its precision. *"On days when crude prices rise mid-session, Excel Energy tends to appreciate in the last two hours of trading. This conclusion is based on a sample of 200 sessions with an accuracy rate of 87%."*

John stared at Vivian in disbelief, marveling at her analytical prowess. *"Wow, she's no slouch!"*

With that exchange, everyone in the room realized that Vivian was there not just to participate, but to dominate. She had already made a profound impression, demonstrating her expertise and determination to leave her mark on the trading room.

Notes:

Securities and Exchange Commission

DECODING THE DESK

Vivian Steele entered the trading room with confident poise. She wore a striking emerald-green sheath dress with a modest V-neckline and knee-length cut, paired with sleek black leather slingback pumps.

Her dark hair fell in loose waves, framing her confident features, with understated makeup enhancing her natural allure. Vivian's presence immediately put John Spinner and Carter Data on alert.

"Good morning! Looks like we have a market with good breath today!" Vivian announces, scanning through the long list of stocks and sectors.

John Spinner, feeling intimidated by Vivian's tough presence, whispers to Carter, *"What did she say? That the market is breathing, that it's alive?"*

Carter shakes his head. *"No, Spinner! Don't be silly. A market with breadth means many stocks are participating in today's rally. Almost all of them are going up with the indices."*

"Ah, got it," John replied, feeling relieved. *"I need you here whenever she shows up to interpret what she's saying. It's like she's speaking a foreign language, all fancy and highbrow, like French!"*

Just then, Victor Fortune enters the room. *"Spinner, you look like a scared stray dog. She doesn't bite, but you wish she would!"*

Laughter erupted among the traders, and John blushed, trying to play off his embarrassment as the group exchanged amused glances, careful not to let Vivian catch wind of their light-hearted banter.

THE QUEEN OF QUANT

In the heart of the financial district, Carter Data was deeply engrossed in his world of stock market charts and graphs. His thick-rimmed glasses sat precariously on his nose as he leaned in, fingers tapping away at the keyboard with precision. With keen eyes scanning the data, he hunted for trading patterns and promising setups. Suddenly, a particular stock, Nexus Dynamics (NXDY), seized his attention.

Carter, intrigued by the potential of NXDY, turned to his colleague, Vivian Steele, a woman known for her sharp financial acumen. *"Miss Steele,"* he inquired, *"what do you think of Nexus Dynamics?"*

Vivian twirled her serpent-shaped ring as if focusing, then without hesitation, launched into a detailed analysis of the company, her voice filled with confidence and expertise. *"It operates within the software sector, boasting a market capitalization of $2 billion. Trading has fluctuated between $22 and $45 over the past year, hitting a peak three weeks ago and a low point in January. Recent sessions indicate an upward trend with moderate fluctuations."*

John Spinner, another colleague within earshot, was astonished by Vivian's rapid-fire recitation of financial data. *"What?"* he exclaimed, his voice laced with disbelief, his flashy and embroidered shirt slightly rumpled as he leaned closer to hear better.

Carter, impressed by Vivian's knowledge, couldn't help but compliment her, *"Vivian, you sound like a computer!"*

Vivian, dressed in a sleek navy-blue power suit that accentuated her confident demeanor, greeted them with a warm smile. *"You can call me 'Vi' if you prefer,"* she said, her voice calm yet authoritative. Laughter rippled through the room at her casual suggestion, breaking the tension and easing John's nerves momentarily.

Bradley Downfall, renowned for his pessimistic market outlook, listened intently before interjecting, *"And what about the risks associated with the stock, Vivian? What's the bearish perspective?"*

Vivian delicately closed her fountain pen, until it was tightly closed, before calmly addressing Bradley's concerns, *"In this particular sector, there is intense competition, which exerts significant pressure on profit margins. Additionally, the recent appointment of a new CEO, who has a track record of instability, adds further complexity."*

Carter, thoroughly impressed by Vivian's comprehensive analysis, exclaimed, *"This is better than any Bloomberg terminal!"*

John, feeling a pang of inadequacy, confessed, *"I should've stayed in school and hit the books harder. I just feel so small compared to all this brainpower around me."*

Ryder Riskmore, injected a touch of humor into the

conversation, *"John, your problem started way back with a lack of breast milk...but at least you turned out handsome!"*

The office erupted in laughter, while John's cheeks flushed with a hint of embarrassment. Despite his self-deprecating remarks, he couldn't help but be drawn to Vivian's intelligence and confidence, secretly admiring her from afar.

LEMONADE AND LAUNCH CODES

Bored at their desks, John and Carter watched their colleague rummaging through her expensive leather bag for a mid-morning snack. Their curiosity was piqued.

"Carter, ask Vivian why she spends her days eating nuts and drinking lemonade?" John Spinner suggested, his voice laced with a hint of intrigue.

"Ask her yourself, John! Don't you have a tongue?" Carter Data retorted, a playful smirk tugging at the corners of his mouth.

"Oh, come on, Carter," John Spinner pleaded, his voice laced with a touch of exasperation. *"You know her presence intimidates me, and I start stuttering. I want to impress her, but first, I need to understand her better, and it's not easy."*

"Well, that's true," Carter Data conceded, his tone softening. *"She's a bit too sophisticated for your taste!"*

With that, John Spinner nudged Carter discreetly, urging him to proceed with his indiscreet question.

Mustering his courage, Carter leaned towards Vivian, his voice laced with curiosity, *"Miss Steele, why nuts and lemon every day? Don't you get bored?"*

Vivian, unfazed by the question, launched into an

explanation, her voice brimming with enthusiasm. *"Nutrients, Carter,"* she began, her eyes sparkling with knowledge. *"Lemon is rich in Vitamin C, strengthens the immune system, aids iron absorption, and has antioxidant powers. Walnuts, on the other hand, are a source of Omega-3, beneficial for the heart and brain. They're also rich in protein and fiber."*

John Spinner, captivated by Vivian's explanation, couldn't contain his excitement, his mouth agape.

Vivian, noticing his enthusiasm, delicately touches up her red lipstick while looking him in the eyes and continues, *"I've optimized my nutrition based on a dietary algorithm I helped develop at NASA for astronaut training."*

John Spinner's jaw dropped, his eyes wide with astonishment. *"NASA?!"* he exclaimed, his voice echoing through the office.

Vivian nodded, a proud smile gracing her lips. *"Yes, I was a NASA researcher for a few years,"* she explained. *"Tomorrow, I'll bring you a miniature Space Shuttle keychain."*

John Spinner's cheeks flushed a rosy hue, while Carter let out a hearty chuckle.

Leaning towards John, Carter whispered, *"You won't even put your keys on it, afraid the friction will scratch it! It's getting better care than most pets!"*

John Spinner, his heart pounding with excitement, couldn't help but agree. Vivian's revelation had opened up a new world of possibilities, igniting a spark of curiosity that would undoubtedly lead to further exploration and connection.

MORNING MIDAS

The atmosphere crackled with tension as Ryder Riskmore slammed his trading console shut and flung his shiny dark blue blazer onto a distant chair. "There I go again," he muttered, running a hand through his hair. *"Start strong, only to fizzle out by the end of the trading session. Break-even, at best, and more often than not, a loss!"*

Maxwell Dither, dressed in khaki trousers and a crisp white shirt, a man whose fingers seemed always ready to type a headline rather than place a trade order, chimed in, *"Classic case of the midday slump, Ryder. You need some supplements. Boost those energy levels!"*

John Spinner, eager to help, chimed in, *"Tell you what, Ryder. My buddy at the corner market, he's from Senegal, swears by this stuff called Moringa. His mom makes these killer recipes, energy cocktails that'd raise the dead!"*

Vivian Steele, the team's resident walking encyclopedia, delicately adjusted her exquisite and refined gemstone necklace before speaking with a faint smile. *"Actually, John, the scientific name is Moringa oleifera. Originally from India, but cultivated in parts of Africa as well. It's renowned for its rich blend of vitamins, minerals, and antioxidants – reputedly excellent for boosting energy levels."*

John flushed a charming shade of crimson, unable to handle even the slightest praise from Miss Steele without turning into a flustered mess.

Ryder, ever the joker, took a jab at Vivian's impressive memory. *"Miss Steele, that computer brain of yours must process more than just market data, huh? You must read a ton. And remember it all too. Unlike some of us who forget everything after a few days."*

Mortimer, the team's elder statesman, had been quietly observing the banter, his tolerance for idle chatter wearing thin with age. *"Ryder,"* he interjected, his voice gravelly but firm, *"The solution to your problem is far simpler than you think, and it doesn't involve any exotic African plants."*

Ryder, ever the skeptic, scoffed. *"Oh yeah? Enlighten me then, Mortimer. What's your miracle cure? Don't tell me you have a secret stash of anti-inflammatory joint juice that doubles as a trading superpower?"* A booming laugh erupted from him, clearly amused by his own joke.

Mortimer, with a stoicism honed by years in the market, countered, *"Forget magic potions, Ryder. Just trade in the morning. Then, for the afternoon? Take a walk, unwind with a book, hit the gym - whatever recharges you. Give your mind a break."*

Ryder's face fell. *"What? And miss out on all the action, the volatility of the closing hour? No way!"*

Mortimer shook his head, a touch of exasperation in his eyes. *"Worse than the blind man, Ryder,"* he sighed, *"is the one who refuses to see."* He crossed himself, a silent plea for Ryder to finally open his eyes to the obvious solution.

LOST IN TRANSLATION

John Spinner's eyes were glued to the screen, watching the HyperJet (HJET) stock plummet dramatically, continuing its downward spiral from the previous trading sessions.

"Carter, look at this!" John exclaimed, his voice laced with a mix of alarm and excitement. *"HyperJet (HJET) is disintegrating! It's the Spring Sale! I can't hold back any longer. I'm going in, I'm buying!"*

Before Carter Data could even respond, Vivian Steele, perched atop her stilettos, interjected her voice, her tone laced with a hint of amusement.

"Are you playing BP, John? That's dangerous and you could get hurt..."

John Spinner, flustered and visibly caught off guard, mumbled his response through gritted teeth.

"No, Miss Steele... Don't worry!"

Not quite grasping the meaning of her comment, but flattered by Vivian's attention, he whispered to Carter, *"Carter, Carter, come here! What did she say? BP? What does that mean?"*

Carter Data, ever the knowledgeable one, replied with a knowing smirk.

"I've never heard the term myself. But from the context, I presume

she's referring to 'Bottom Picker'. It refers to a trader who consistently tries to buy assets at their lowest possible price, attempting to time the market perfectly by buying just as prices are reaching their lowest point, or 'bottoming out'."

At this point, Victor Fortune, who had been eavesdropping on the conversation, couldn't resist joining in, his voice dripping with sarcasm.

"Nonsense, Spinner. Vivian was talking about her dream last night... She meant to say, 'Bedroom Provocateur'! I think she's falling for you!"

Carter burst into laughter, so hard he almost wet his pants. John, increasingly confused, couldn't decide whether to laugh along or take Victor's revelation seriously. Either way, he completely forgot about his intended HyperJet (HJET) trade, and in a sense, he had already won the day.

A SEISMIC TRADE

The day was progressing calmly on Wall Street when suddenly the ticker flashed, *"Major Earthquake in Northern China: Qinghai with Damaged Infrastructure."* Vivian Steele leapt like an Olympic gymnast and fired off an order on the keyboard with lightning speed.

Maxwell Dither, in his usual eloquence, commented, *"That area is very prone to seismic activity; it's where India collides with the rest of Asia."* John Spinner didn't hear Maxwell's geology lesson, his eyes glued to Viviane.

"Carter, did you notice that as soon as the headline appeared on the monitors, Vi immediately placed an order? What did she do? Ask her!" John urged.

"There you go, John! So outgoing about almost everything and so shy with Miss Steele! Why, I wonder..." Carter replied.

"Come on! She definitely did something smart, but what?" John persisted.

Maxwell Dither looked at the quotes and exclaimed in surprise, *"ArcadiaX Gaming (DIAX) is down 27%! Strange...could it be a glitch?"*

Vivian quickly explained, *"ArcadiaX produces 90% of its consoles* around Qinghai. With the destruction that an earthquake like this causes to factories and road infrastructure, they won't have consoles available in stores for Christmas. Production was already slightly delayed and now the holiday season is irretrievably lost."

"Miss Steele, how do you know that ArcadiaX Gaming produces 90% of its consoles in Qinghai?!" Carter asked, amazed.

"I read it in the annual report. All the information is there."

"And the order you placed was related to that?" Carter continued.

"Yes, I was quick...one of the first to react or maybe the first. I managed to short sell 50,000 shares before the sell-off. I've got a good open profit on this position, capturing almost the entire sell-off. My week is made," Vivian responded confidently.

John whispered, "The week? I wish that were my entire year..."

Mortimer Sagecroft, who had listened with interest to the entire interaction, commented, "Well, I admire Maxwell's knowledge and broad cultural understanding. He knew Qinghai is in China's seismic zone and the geological reason for it. However, from a trading standpoint, that information had no value... Miss Steele, on the other hand, applied knowledge she had gathered and used it immediately upon seeing the headline. Preparation and knowledge truly pay off." As Joe Paterno wisely put it, "The will to win is important, but the will to prepare is vital.'"

John, visibly excited by Viviane's performance, threw at Maxwell, "Hey, Dither! Looks like you've been reading the wrong books!" Carter and John laughed, leaving Maxwell embarrassed.

Maxwell quickly slipped into his British fabric blazer and retorted, *"Your ignorance must be worth a fortune!"* He stepped outside for some fresh air, certain that his big trade was just waiting for the right mix of technicals, fundamentals, and his own risk tolerance. Maxwell had faith, even if he stood alone in it.

SLIM PROFITS

SlimGenix (SGNX) stocks are on the rise once again, and Ryder Riskmore had caught the upswing.

"Look at SlimGenix (SGNX) stocks," exclaimed Maxwell Dither. *"They're climbing again!"*

"They've surged 123% year to date!" Carter Data exclaimed, adjusting his glasses with a scholarly air. *"I'm not entirely convinced if it's just a passing trend or if they've genuinely developed a game-changing product. We'll need to see if the company's underlying fundamentals can substantiate this stock appreciation over time..."*

Bradley Downfall interjected cynically, *"This is nothing but a fleeting frenzy! It'll enjoy a brief stint as a darling of Wall Street, only to inevitably disappoint with lackluster earnings and projections, crashing hard thereafter. It's a tired cycle that repeats itself endlessly in this market. It baffles me how traders still fall for these dubious promoters."*

Meanwhile, Carter continued, undeterred by Bradley's pessimism. *"Ryder has been long since the low $20s. It's at $42... or rather, $43 now. It just keeps going up!"*

Maxwell chuckled, *"The stock itself is gaining weight! What's Ryder's reasoning for being so optimistic about the stocks?"*

Carter explained, *"He says he's done his research—talking to a few gym buddies who are trying to lose weight. He's convinced that SlimGenix (SGNX) pills are very effective, paired with highly appealing marketing. And because he believes in it, he's holding onto his position..."*

John Spinner chimed in skeptically, *"Sounds too simple..."*

Carter smirked, adding another layer to Ryder's conviction. *"Oh, and besides that, Ryder mentioned the other day he peeked into Miss Steele's trash can and saw a box of SlimTech pills. Given her striking appearance and nutritional knowledge, he's even more convinced of the stock's potential and doubled down on his position."*

Bradley, ever the voice of caution, warned, *"Don't get caught up in the hype, Spinner. It's just a passing trend, a hype that will cost those half-baked speculators dearly... the stocks will reverse and plummet to levels that smell like insolvency!"*

John chuckled at Bradley's unwavering skepticism. *"You never hold back, do you?"*

Carter smiled, shaking his head affectionately. *"That's just Bradley being... Bradley!"*

The group shared a laugh, enjoying the banter and camaraderie even as they debated the future of SlimGenix (SGNX) stocks in the volatile world of Wall Street.

THE BAGEL SHOP TRADE

On the day of Aquagen Solutions (AQUA)'s earnings announcement, everyone stayed late for the after-hours session to witness the real-time release of results. Seemingly, no one held positions in the stock, but in reality, that wasn't entirely true.

As the countdown to the announcement began, anticipation filled the room. John Spinner, always optimistic, grinned and exclaimed, *"Let the fireworks begin! It's going to be like the closing show at DisneyWorld!"* His excitement was palpable.

Maxwell Dither, the eternal skeptic, shook his head. *"This type of stock attracts nothing but gamblers, gunslingers. Earnings for this are like playing the lottery. I'd never touch a stock like this,"* he asserted confidently. Under his breath, John muttered, *"Not in any way..."*

Maxwell continued, his tone a mix of disbelief and disdain. *"Aquagen Solutions (AQUA) shares just surged 40% last week, it's insane!"*

Carter Data, the group's junior analyst, contributed some numbers to the discussion. *"I've got the expected volatility for these earnings. Options are pricing in a 30% move up or down with the earnings release,"* he said, displaying detailed charts on his screen.

Mortimer Sagecroft, the voice of experience, cautioned, *"Those on the wrong side will learn a hard lesson. If they're heavily leveraged, they might blow up their trading accounts."* His words hung heavily in the air, a stark reminder of the risks involved.

"Where's Miss Steele when we need her most?" John Spinner asked. *"If she were here, I'd ask for her take on AQUA's prospects... Maybe hitch a ride on her insights, things have been tough lately..."*

Carter Data replied, *"You know she rarely trades on Wednesday afternoons. She's usually doing pro bono work for a nature conservation foundation."*

Suddenly, the room buzzed with activity as the results flashed across the ticker. Earnings printed just slightly below consensus, and the stock unexpectedly plummeted 35% in an instant. The reaction was swift and intense.

Ryder Riskmore celebrated as if his team had scored a goal, leaving everyone staring at him in confusion. Maxwell, always quick to question, asked, *"What's going on, Ryder? Are you having a seizure?"*

With a triumphant smile, Ryder responded, *"I'm cashing in big time! I had a massive short position* on AQUA, and with this drop, I'm making a killing!"* His excitement was contagious, though it left some feeling a bit envious.

John Spinner looked at him, surprised. *"And you didn't tell anyone? I could have jumped in! I could really use a win..."*

Maxwell, never one to miss an opportunity for his classic skepticism, inquired, *"What was your rationale? Were you just playing the lottery?"*

Ryder, enjoying the spotlight, began to explain. *"Jose, the Colombian guy at the café across the street, told me this morning he was hyped about Aquagen's stock. He knew it was going to move big today, but didn't know why exactly."*

Raising an eyebrow, Maxwell asked, *"Jose from the Coffee & Bagel shop?"*

"Yeah!" Ryder continued. *"He mentioned all his buddies had been buying the stock in recent weeks. It was all the talk in his neighborhood. So, Carter had shown me a study suggesting crowded trades often burst, so I took a shot."*

Impressed, Carter nodded. *"Risk-taking, but well played! Theory meets practice, nicely done."*

Ryder had turned street smarts into a memorable trade, transforming an ordinary day into an extraordinary one.

* A short position is when an investor sells a borrowed asset, expecting its price to drop, so they can buy it back later at a lower price for a profit.

CURSED ON WALL STREET

John found himself unusually subdued. As the clock ticked past 11 am, his trading desk remained devoid of any transactions, a stark departure from his usual flurry of activity.

His colleagues, sensing his unusual demeanor, couldn't resist poking fun. *"What's with the long face, Spinner?"* quipped Carter Data, a sly grin spreading across his face. *"The market's more active than you today! Need a shot of espresso to wake you up?"*

Laughter rippled through the office, John being the frequent target of their lighthearted jabs. But amidst the teasing, there was genuine concern for their typically energetic colleague.

John Spinner, his brow furrowed, spilled the beans on his morning disaster. *"You won't believe what went down this morning,"* he started, his voice with a touch of unease. *"I'm rounding the corner, almost at the office, and bam! I bump into this homeless dude chilling there, asking for handouts. And in my rush, I accidentally boot his cardboard box full of coins, sending them flying all over the damn street."*

Ryder, always playful, couldn't resist teasing John. *"Don't tell me you were lost in thoughts, imagining Miss Steele in a revealing bikini with a Mojito* in hand, lounging on a Caribbean beach?"*

Everyone chuckled at Ryder's remark, but Maxwell noticed that

John was still quite shaken by the incident...

Maxwell Dither, seemingly concerned, asked, *"And you've been pondering this mishap all morning? Lost in deep contemplation, are we?"*

John shook his head, looking serious. *"It's not just that. It's what the old man dropped on me after I said sorry. He looks at me dead serious and goes, 'May money flee from you as the devil flees from the cross!'"*

A hush fell over the office as John's words hung in the air, the weight of the curse settling upon them. Mortimer, the office sage, offered a consoling pat on John's shoulder. *"Well, consider it a blessing in disguise, John. At least today you'll avoid your usual trading mishaps. Maybe it'll give you a chance to think twice before opening a position."*

Maxwell, always the chief teaser, chimed in, *"Don't worry, Victor knows a lucky charm seller who can whip up a potion to reverse your misfortune."*

Victor Fortune, a self-proclaimed expert in all things mystical, couldn't resist injecting his trademark humor. *"Or you could try rubbing garlic paste all over your body as an anti-evil eye ointment. It's sure to make you so fragrant that Miss Steele might just invite you to dinner!"*

Laughter filled the room, momentarily lifting the gloom that had settled over them. Despite the lack of trades and the lingering unease of John's curse, the camaraderie and lighthearted banter of the office provided a much-needed respite from the pressures of the financial world.

* *Mojito, a refreshing cocktail made with white rum, lime juice, mint leaves, sugar, and soda water, typically served over ice.*

THE SLOW DAY SAGA: HOW THE TICKER CAME TO BE

Wednesday afternoons often dragged in the office when Miss Steele was away, off at a nature conservation foundation. John, visibly affected by her absence, unwittingly infected the rest of the group with his melancholy, casting an unusual lethargy over the room. Adding to the doldrums, the market was sluggish, and the ticker displayed no signs of activity.

Carter Data sighed, *"The ticker is barely moving. What a dull trading day. Does anyone actually know the history behind this ticker?"*

Mortimer Sagecroft replied, *"Ah, that's an old tale."*

Ryder Riskmore added, *"Tell us. Help us pass the time. With this market in a coma, we have nothing to trade."*

Mortimer Sagecroft began, *"The origins of the ticker go back to the mid-19th century. It's tied to the invention of the telegraph, which allowed for rapid transmission of information over long distances. This technology was quickly adapted to relay stock prices across the country."*

Just then, John Spinner, who had nodded off, accidentally banged his head on the coffee table.

Carter Data chuckled, *"So, Spinner? Did Mortimer's story knock you out?"*

John Spinner rubbed his head, half-awake, *"What story?"* He felt his head for a bump. *"It's this market that's putting me to sleep."*

Mortimer continued, *"Moving on... A man named Edward Graham, an employee of the American Telegraph Company, modified a telegraph to print stock quotes using abbreviated symbols on a paper roll. And voilà, the ticker was born!"*

Carter Data exclaimed, *"Brilliant, professor!"*

The group laughed, finding a way to liven up the sluggish afternoon session with tales of the ticker's inception.

CHESS MOVES AND SWORDPLAY

In the midst of a rare quiet spell at the brokerage, Ryder Riskmore leaned back in his chair, breaking the silence with a casual remark to his colleagues, his dark, well-dressed attire exuding a hint of flashiness without being ostentatious.

"On my way in this morning," Ryder began with a grin, his eyes animated, *"I spotted this kid tearing it up on a BMX. It took me back to my own BMX days—those races were everything to me. Remember this scar?"* He chuckled, running his hand over a faint mark on his forehead. *"Anyway, what about you guys? What sports did you play growing up?"*

Carter Data, the numbers whiz with a penchant for precision, chimed in first. *"Nice one, Ryder. BMX suits your style perfectly. As for me, sports weren't exactly my thing. I was more of a Math Olympics kind of guy—spent more time with numbers than on the field."*

Ryder couldn't help but tease. *"Carter, you're a true nerd!"*

Mortimer Sagecroft, the seasoned sailor with a fondness for the sea, reminisced next. *"I used to sail with my father off Newport, Rhode Island. Those were the days—nothing like the open water and that sense of freedom."*

Maxwell Dither, known for his bookish habits and an affinity for literature, nodded in agreement. *"Absolutely, Mortimer. Your story* reminds me of Hemingway's 'The Old Man and the Sea.' It's one of my favorites. I wasn't exactly a star athlete. My folks put me in golf lessons, but it was more about keeping me occupied while they played. I'd sneak a book into my bag and find a quiet spot after a few swings."

Vivian Steele, known for her sharp intellect and competitive spirit, joined the conversation in a sleek black dress that emphasized her confident presence. *"Chess and fencing were my passions. Chess taught me strategy, and fencing sharpened my reflexes while managing my competitive drive. It paid off—I won a silver at the Youth Olympic Games, the YOG."*

Ryder grinned at Vivian. *"No sword these days, but your presence still strikes fear."*

Vivian laughed softly. *"Ryder, you know I'm as harmless as a kitten."*

Victor also shared his childhood pursuit. *"Sports weren't my forte either. I was all about poker from about fourteen. Cleaned up at those weekend games around my neighborhood—luck and smarts kept me in the chips for years."*

John Spinner, ever the rogue with a flair for adventure, interjected with a sly smirk. *"Victor, now I don't feel so bad sharing my childhood 'sport.' I used to swipe oranges from the grocers in Queens and sprint home! Talk about an adrenaline rush."*

Carter chuckled. *"Only you, Spinner."*

Vivian flashed John a warm smile, her black stilettos dangling sensually from her toes. *"John,"* she purred, her voice rich and teasing, *"your adventurous spirit is absolutely charming."* Her gaze lingered on him, a playful sparkle in her eyes, as her shoe swayed rhythmically, adding a touch of flirtation to her compliment.

Spinner blushed slightly, nervously toying with his flashy gold chain necklace, while Ryder teased him further. *"This guy's gonna lose sleep tonight!"*

The office buzzed with their shared memories and laughter, a brief respite from the frenetic pace of trading. Each story painted a portrait of their diverse personalities and backgrounds, blending into a mosaic of camaraderie in the high-stakes world they navigated every day.

MISS STEELE'S SECRET

Right after the market closed, Ryder approached John Spinner and Carter, saying, *"You guys won't believe what I saw in Miss Steele's bag today..."*

John reacted as if he'd been jabbed with a needle, jumping in his chair. *"What? What?"*

Ryder milked the moment for drama, taking his time before saying, *"Some shiny metal handcuffs..."*

Carter, in a tone not quite his own but caught up in the moment, asked, *"Is she working the night shift as a cop?"* Ryder and Carter burst into uncontrollable laughter, while John sat there stunned and speechless.

Turning to Carter, Ryder remarked, *"I think one of these days Miss Steele will handcuff John to the trading desk and teach him to trade after dark!"* laughing uncontrollably afterward.

"You dirty lowlifes!" John muttered as he stormed out of the office, visibly disturbed by what he had just heard. What dangerous schemes had she been plotting? Who is Miss Steele beyond the super trader she portrays herself to be during the day?

TICK-TOCK TRADES

The atmosphere buzzed with conversation at the brokerage, and Spinner's remark sparked curiosity.

"Hey, have you ever noticed," John Spinner began, *"that all the big-time traders sport a killer watch?"*

Maxwell Dither, sharp-witted and polished, nodded in agreement. *"Absolutely, John. It's a symbol of old money, of success. An expensive automatic watch always looks good, giving the wearer status and class."*

Mortimer Sagecroft, the elder statesman of the trio, glanced at the wall clock. *"Speaking of time, it's the opening bell."*

Maxwell turned to Mortimer with curiosity. *"Mortimer, what watch do you wear?"*

Mortimer smiled faintly. *"The same one as always. A manual wind watch that belonged to my father."*

John couldn't help but crack a joke. *"One of those that's only right twice a day, Mortimer?"*

Mortimer chuckled. *"Not at all, John. It's accurate and precise, made in Switzerland."*

John's eyes lit up with excitement. *"I spotted one at the boutique* on the avenue. It's a bit steep, but in market terms, it's like pocketing a quick $1 profit from a 2,000-share trade. Easy pickings for an afternoon's hustle!"

Maxwell raised an eyebrow. *"That kind of thinking can be very costly, John. You might make a hasty trade, not that you're not used to it!"* He laughed heartily.

Mortimer leaned forward, his tone serious. *"Spinner, forget about the watch immediately! Trying to fund your watch through the market could cost you the value of a car. You'd be better off taking your bills, soaking them in gasoline, and setting them on fire!"*

Maxwell interjected with a playful quip. *"Well, in winter, that little bonfire might warm us up..."*

Ryder Riskmore chimed in, *"But I think I know what's going on here... John wants to impress Vivian with a classy watch. Even if it means risking financial ruin to buy it with money 'gifted' by the market!"*

John, playing the wise guy, responded, *"Alright, cool. I'll hold back this time. I'll settle for half a watch from the market... I'll stick with a 1,000-share trade!"*

Mortimer shook his head in mock exasperation. *"You guys never learn. As for me, that's enough for today. I'm out for an afternoon walk."*

JUICY TRADE

John Spinner had read a headline on the front page of The Financial Tribune a few weeks ago, predicting that the orange harvest in Florida would be affected by adverse weather and that prices could skyrocket by summer. With the help of his broker, he set up a speculative position in Florida Orange futures, hoping this meteorological disaster would cause orange prices to soar, resulting in a rare profitable deal.

Upon arriving at the trading room, he receives a notification about the approaching expiration of his futures contract and the need to close his position. He closely watches the quotes, anxiously looking for the price of Florida Orange futures.

"75 bid / 102 ask? Are you kidding me? What kind of spread is this? I can only sell at 75? There's zero liquidity here! How is the spread this wide?"

Carter Data, calmly at his desk, asks, *"At what price did you enter?"*

John replies, *"I got in at 100. I wanted to sell at 101-102, but not a single trade has gone through for hours... and now I got a notice to close the contract today or I'll have to go to delivery? What delivery? Sounds like I'm running a food truck!"*

Maxwell: *"Yes, indeed, the Florida Orange futures show no bids at all. The market depth looks more like Gukanjima Island*."*

John Spinner: *"Stop with the stories, Dither! I have a serious problem on my hands. How am I going to get out of this position without taking a huge loss?"*

Mortimer Sagecroft, passing by on his slow walk to his mid-morning tea, stops next to John. *"It's the problem with trading assets with little or no liquidity, John. Plus, it's a futures contract you let get too close to the first notice date. Now, liquidity is minimal, and the spreads are wide."*

John Spinner: *"First notice? Damn, Mortimer. It sounds like a court notice; it scares me."*

Mortimer, with the patience of Job, reassures John by explaining the terminology used in the futures market. *"The first notice on a futures contract is when the seller of the contract must notify the buyer of their intention to deliver the underlying asset. Or, in this case, you would have to physically pick up the oranges corresponding to the contract you purchased."*

John, stunned and frightened, asks, *"Picking up the oranges? How... by truck? Where from?"*

Viviane Steele approached John, exuding the essence of spring in her outfit. Her attire featured floral patterns, complemented by 7 cm high-heeled sandals that accentuated her elegant stride. A hint of citrus-scented perfume lingered around her, adding to her allure as she addressed John.

"If you let the first notice slip by," she began, her voice smooth yet

tinged with concern, *"you'll find yourself having to collect a ton of oranges from a warehouse in the Greater Miami Area. Doesn't sound like a smart move, does it, John?"*

Ryder, more amused than ever with the mess Spinner has gotten into, quips, *"Don't worry, we can help you pick up the merchandise! I know a friend of the Mayor, and maybe we can convince him to organize something like the Tomatina**, but with oranges! What do you think? It would be fun!"*

Carter: *"Miami Beach would be a great spot for a quick getaway, John. Maybe you can talk Miss Steele into joining you. I can already see you there, the Orange King or just O.K., with a real queen by your side!"*

John Spinner: *"O.K.? I'm totally K.O.!!!"*

* *Gukanjima Island, off Nagasaki's coast, was a thriving coal mining site during Japan's industrialization but has been abandoned since the 1970s. Its densely packed concrete buildings create a stark, eerie atmosphere, likened to a ghost town rising from the sea.*

** *The Tomatina is a renowned festival in Buñol, Spain, where people throw tomatoes at each other in a lively and colorful event held annually in August.*

THE PINK BOTTLE

John Spinner strolled into the office, swinging a bright pink water bottle. Carter Data noticed and couldn't resist a comment.

"Hey, Spinner! What's with the huge bottle? Planning to stay hydrated for a week?"

John smirked. *"My new nutritionist says a well-hydrated brain works twice as well."*

Maxwell Dither, always ready with a quote, chimed in. *"As Goethe said, 'All is born of water, all is sustained by water.'"*

John unknowingly revealed his ignorance to Maxwell. *"Looks like my nutritionist and yours are on the same page, Maxwell."*

Maxwell, with a dry sense of humor, replied, *"If only the dead could confirm that."*

Before more banter could ensue, Ryder Riskmore added his own quip. *"Hey, Spinner! Just try not to drown in losses!"*

Laughter filled the office, leaving Spinner puzzled by the sudden shift in tone.

SPLIT SAGA

John hurried into the trading room, already late for the morning session. He quickly scanned his monitor, only to freeze in shock.

"Yo, what's up with Fusion NanoDevices (FUNA)?" John blurted out, his voice tinged with panic. "The stocks are tanking 90%! I've got nearly all my cash in FUNA. How's that even happening?!"

Carter, relaxed because he didn't hold any position in the stock, leaned over. *"Hold on, John. It looks like they did a stock split."*

"A stock-strip? What the heck?" John's confusion was obvious.

Ryder Riskmore seized the opportunity to tease, bursting into laughter. *"Hey, Spinner, I already know where you were last night, you sly dog! No use pretending otherwise!"*

John felt a twinge of embarrassment, realizing his slip might have revealed more than he intended.

"Chill out, Ryder!" John cut in quickly, cheeks turning a bit red. *"Quit with the jokes. Miss Steele might hear and get the wrong idea. Keep it clean."*

Ignoring the banter, Mortimer stepped forward, ready to clarify. *"John, a stock split means..."*

John's mind, always on overdrive, cut off Mortimer. *"Oh, I get it, now! Like a banana split! Speaking of which, I could really use one right now..."*

Carter chuckled, shaking his head. *"When it comes to sweets, John, you're the real expert!"*

Mortimer resumed, his patience akin to a seasoned educator. *"Listen, John. In a 10-1 stock split, like this one, shareholders receive ten shares for every one they held before. At the same time, the stock price adjusts downwards by a factor of ten. That's why it appears to have dropped 90%. But in reality, the total value of your investment remains unchanged."*

The realization hit John. *"So, instead of a hundred shares, I now have a thousand? Feels like I've leveled up as a trader."*

Vivian approached with her black stilettos echoing on the floor with every confident step she took. *"Studies indicate that in the short term, stock splits often appeal to small investors who prefer holding a greater number of shares, even while the overall value remains unchanged."*

Maxwell, always ready with a metaphor, chimed in. *"It's like the placebo effect in the stock market."*

Vivian nodded in agreement. *"Exactly, Maxwell. Nicely articulated."*

With the room now hushed, Vivian glided away, her stilettos punctuating the silence with each precise step. John felt a jolt as he fixated on the sharp clack of her heels against the polished wood floor, a reminder of her commanding presence in both the world of markets and his own swirling thoughts.

MARKET BLUES: WHEN PRISON SEEMS PREFERABLE

After yet another trade closed at a loss, John Spinner slumped in his chair, the weight of disappointment palpable in his demeanor. *"This is going from bad to worse. It's my sixth consecutive losing trade,"* he muttered, his eyes fixed grimly on the flickering numbers on his computer screen.

Mortimer, seeing John's sadness, approached him with a sympathetic expression. *"You need to figure out what went wrong, John. Look at your trades, try to understand why you lost. Remember how teachers used to do it right after giving tests back? They'd go over the mistakes with us to help us learn."*

John, in his typically carefree style, confessed, *"Mortimer, when I close a trade, I'm already itching to jump into the next one. I thrive on the adrenaline rush of making a new move. I'm not one to dwell on losses. And my math teacher? You know what she used to say? 'You're gonna end up in prison as an adult, Johnny!'"*

Ryder, who had been attentively listening from his desk, couldn't resist needling Spinner with a sly grin. *"Well, that's something. You've certainly exceeded your teacher's expectations!"*

A brief silence followed as John's expression turned introspective. *"Yeah, I might not be in jail, but with the way things are going in the markets and my finances looking bleak, at least in prison, I'd have a roof over my head and three meals a day,"* he said with a half-joking tone, revealing a hint of resignation mixed with gallows humor.

Miss Steele, stirring her espresso with measured calmness and crossing her legs with elegant poise, felt genuine sympathy for John during his rough patch. Her comforting smile was genuine as she spoke softly, *"John, you've always been so kind to me. If you ever found yourself in prison, I would visit you without hesitation. I might even bring along some homemade cookies to lift your spirits."*

Ryder leaned in closer to John, a mischievous glint in his eyes and a playful smirk on his lips. Lowering his voice conspiratorially, he teased, *"Don't start getting ideas, John. Her visit wouldn't be a conjugal one, just so you know."* His playful tone carried a hint of camaraderie mixed with teasing banter, a familiar dynamic between colleagues in the trading room.

ANACONDA GREEN

Spinner watched the terminals flash green and red, then turned to Mortimer, the old fox who knew everything about financial markets and their history. *"Mortimer, why do we see green when markets rally and red when they dive?"*

Mortimer relished these impromptu lessons. Rising from his chair, he briskly buttoned his tweed blazer and strode among the trading desks with the air of a seasoned professor delivering a lecture. *"The association of green with up markets and red with down markets stems from cultural symbolism and practical visibility. In many cultures, green is associated with positive concepts like growth and prosperity, while red signifies danger and loss. This color coding can be traced back to traffic lights where green means 'go' and red means 'stop.' In financial markets, green indicates prices going up and red indicates prices going down."*

Ryder, listening attentively, added his two cents. *"Yes, but there are exceptions. Sometimes I trade Asian markets during my insomnia. In China and Japan, for example, red means rising and green means falling."*

Mortimer, impressed by Ryder's insight, nodded. *"Excellent, Ryder. A perfect example of learning by doing. In some Asian markets, the color conventions are reversed. Red is associated with good fortune and prosperity, so it indicates rising prices, while green indicates falling prices. Cultural significance plays a major role in these variations."*

John Spinner, delighted with the explanation, grinned. *"Now I've got a story to tell at the bar later..."*

Miss Steele interjected gracefully, *"Look!"* She delicately wiggled her fingers, her hands adorned with impeccably manicured nails, each movement exuding elegance and a hint of playful teasing. Her fingers moved with a natural grace, commanding attention effortlessly as they danced in the air. *"When the indices are trending up like they are now, I opt for a dark green nail polish. If the markets are on a downturn, I switch to red. It helps me stay mindful of where to place my focus in trading. Ryder, I'm surprised you didn't catch that,"* Vivian teased.

Ryder and Vivian exchange glances, a spark in the air.

John Spinner doesn't even register the interaction between the two, his mind consumed by the idea that a single color on a desk mere feet away could reshape his tumultuous trading career, *"Damn, that's the holy grail of technical indicators! Just gotta check your hands to know which side of the market I'm playing!"*

Ryder sidled up to John, aiming to temper his enthusiasm. *"Careful, Spinner. That green on Miss Steele's hands? It's not your average shade—it's deep, dark, with subtle black undertones, like the skin of an anaconda slithering through the jungle. And you might just find yourself entangled as her next prey!"* he teased, a knowing smirk playing on his lips.

A nearby trader mimicked the sound of a snake, then said

"Anaconda Green..." and burst into laughter, realizing that every conversation about Miss Steele inevitably centered around John's unwitting captivation by her irresistible charm.

COPPER GLOW

As the trading session approached its final stretch on Wall Street, tension mounted when the screens abruptly flashed: *"Breaking News: Assassination Attempt on Esteban Rojas..."* Viviane Steele's eyes darted to the screens for a fleeting moment before her intense focus returned to her trading station. With swift precision, she unleashed a flurry of orders, each keystroke echoing the urgency of the unfolding situation.

Carter Data, who was nearby, queried sharply, *"Who in the world is Esteban Rojas?"*

John Spinner shot back, *"Sounds like a Mexican cartel beef or something."*

Observing Vivian's swift actions after the headline, Carter inquired with intensity, *"Miss Steele, who exactly is Esteban Rojas? And how does this headline affect the trading action?"*

Miss Steele, seated at her trading desk in a black pencil skirt and pristine white silk blouse, epitomized poise under pressure. Her perfectly defined eyebrows framed eyes that darted across multiple screens, while her sharply cut stiletto heels tapped rhythmically against the floor. With an emphatic wave of her hand and a silent *"Wait"* mouthed from her bold red lips, Viviane signaled her focus. She had already opened massive positions, strategically poised to capitalize on the market movements triggered by the headline.

Meanwhile, Maxwell had time to open the developing news story and added, *"Esteban Rojas is the charismatic leader of Chilean mine workers. He's a communist negotiating for higher wages and better working conditions. This could impact copper prices and companies that own copper mines."*

Carter persisted, *"Miss Steele? Enlighten us."*

Viviane paused for a moment, adjusting her skirt to ensure the lace of her stockings remained discreetly hidden. She then spoke with the calm authority of a seasoned Wall Street trader. *"This headline is likely to drive up copper prices and boost the stocks of copper mining companies in Peru and Australia. Esteban Rojas is a revered figure among Chilean copper miners, who will likely strike and halt production. Consequently, I immediately bought copper futures and shares of Outback Copper Corp. (OCC) and Peruvian Copper Resources (PCOP) as soon as the headline broke, managing to secure an early entry price. Speed of execution is critical in these situations. Now, with these initial profits, I can strategically manage the position moving forward."*

John Spinner asked, *"Why those choices, Viv?"*

"With copper production in Chile expected to take a significant hit, there will be less supply, which typically translates to higher commodity prices. Who stands to gain while Chilean mines are offline?" Vivian replied thoughtfully, her hand deftly sketching a diagram in her notebook with a sleek fountain pen. The fine nib glided smoothly across the page, leaving a trail of deep indigo ink.

Each stroke was precise and deliberate, reflecting her meticulous analysis of market dynamics.

John sported a boldly patterned shirt in shades of salmon and vibrant blue, paired with a chain around his neck and a mane of voluminous, curly hair. His flashy ensemble exuded a unique charm that catered to a specific taste.

"Yo, Viv, this is getting way over our heads," John remarked, gesturing to the complex topic at hand.

Vivian leans back gracefully, skillfully pinning up her hair. *"The Australian and Peruvian copper miners. After Chile, the world's largest copper producer, countries like Peru and Australia are next in line. Having meticulously analyzed the earnings reports of nearly every major copper company worldwide, I expect these two to benefit the most from the market's response."*

Mortimer Sagecroft interjected with a refined air, *"This is the intersection of preparation and opportunity, my dear. Those countless hours devoted to poring over research, annual reports, and commodity analyses yield dividends, not just in the future, but in the present moment. Splendid foresight, Miss Steele."*

John Spinner and Carter Data looked on in disbelief. Carter harbored aspirations of becoming a trader as astute as Vivian, realizing that beyond meticulously studying every traded asset and its interrelations, he needed to cultivate quick reflexes and unwavering composure to seize aggressive opportunities without delay. In the trading room, the adage *"time is money"* resonated more profoundly than anywhere else.

UNVEILING VIVIAN STEELE: THE NAMING JOURNEY

Choosing character names is an important aspect for fiction writers. Here are the reasons why I thought Vivian Steele was the right name:

Sophistication and Authority: "Vivian" suggests sophistication and intelligence, while "Steele" conveys strength and authority. Together, they create a name that reflects the character's demeanor and presence in the financial world.

Memorability: Vivian Steele is a name that is easy to remember and stands out, which is crucial for a character who plays a significant role in the story.

Alignment with Character Traits: The name Vivian Steele aligns well with the character's traits such as analytical genius, strategic thinking, and mental toughness. It embodies the qualities that define her persona.

Flirting Potential: Additionally, the name Vivian Steele carries a subtle allure, hinting at the character's intriguing and possibly flirtatious nature. It suggests a depth and charisma that can captivate others in the story, adding another layer to her personality.

Overall, Vivian Steele was chosen because it encapsulates the essence of the character and resonates with the story's themes and settings.

ABOUT THE AUTHOR

Henrique M. Simões

Henrique M. Simões is a seasoned futures trader with over two decades of expertise in decoding the intricate world of short-term trading patterns. From the early stages of his career, Henrique was captivated by the dynamic nature of financial markets, leading him on a relentless pursuit of knowledge and mastery in the art of trading.

With a wealth of hands-on experience accumulated over 20-plus years, Henrique has honed his skills in navigating the complexities of the market, specializing in short-term trading strategies that require a keen understanding of market dynamics and swift decision-making. His unique insights into trading patterns have not only withstood the test of time but have consistently yielded success in the fast-paced world of futures trading.

BOOKS BY THIS AUTHOR

Trading Tales: Adventures In The Stock Market - Volume 1

This book is a collection of funny stories about traders who gather at a brokerage to conduct business in the stock market. Rivalries, conflicts, and envy take hold of the characters involved in picturesque episodes.

Inspired by actual individuals I've encountered throughout my career in trading, spanning both brokerage firms and hedge funds, these stories provide glimpses into the colorful characters that populate the trading world.

From seasoned veterans to ambitious newcomers, the brokerage is a melting pot of diverse personalities, each with their own unique approach to the market. Amidst the buzz of trading terminals and ringing phones, rivalries simmer, conflicts flare up, and envy rears its head, driving the narrative forward with palpable energy and tension.

Whether it's the cutthroat competition for lucrative deals or the camaraderie forged over shared victories and defeats, these tales offer a delightful glimpse into the human drama that unfolds behind the scenes of the financial markets. So sit back, relax, and enjoy the ride as we journey into the world of trading.

Trading Tales: The Ticker Never Stops - Volume 2

This book is the second part of a series of humorous tales about traders congregating at a brokerage to navigate the complexities of the stock market. Within these stories, the characters find themselves entangled in rivalries, conflicts, and bouts of envy, painting vivid scenes of their experiences.

Drawing from my encounters with real individuals throughout my career in trading, spanning various brokerage firms and hedge funds, these narratives shed light on the diverse cast of characters that inhabit the trading realm.

From seasoned veterans to eager newcomers, the brokerage serves as a melting pot of personalities, each bringing their own unique trading style to the table. Amidst the hustle and bustle of trading terminals and incessant phone calls, tensions rise, conflicts erupt, and envy bubbles to the surface, infusing the storyline with a tangible sense of excitement and suspense.

Whether it's the fierce competition for lucrative deals or the bonds forged through shared triumphs and setbacks, these tales provide an engaging peek into the human dynamics unfolding behind the scenes of financial markets. So, kick back, unwind, and immerse yourself in the journey through the world of trading.

Trading Course: How To Become A Consistently Winning Trader

Highly successful and professional futures trader and economist Henrique M. Simões has created this no-nonsense course based upon his vast knowledge, almost two decades of experience, and razor-sharp expertise. It focuses on helping you obtain a unique trading signature and endless successful trades throughout your career.

The book progresses through six chapters, each building upon the last to help you develop a deep foundation to boost your trading career in order to achieve optimum levels of success.

Inside, you will learn how to develop a trading system and discover which trading techniques should be included in trading methodology. You'll also learn about the psychological aspect of trading and how you must treat your trading activities as a business.

Ultimately, this book guides you to begin creating your success without the extensive trial and error periods that thousands of other traders have endured. Every trader knows there is money to be made, and Simões's course will urge you not to attempt to predict the markets but rather follow the techniques and guidelines offered to achieve consistent winning trades.

700+ Insights To Mastering Short-Term Trading: Lifelong Lessons From A Seasoned Trader

Dive into the world of short-term trading with '700+ Insights to Mastering Short-Term Trading - Lifelong Lessons from a Seasoned Trader,' a comprehensive guide crafted by a seasoned trader for aspiring, developing, and expert traders alike. This book offers a treasure trove of trading wisdom, delivering concise yet powerful one or two-sentence reflections and advice that span every facet of a trader's journey. From conquering the learning curve to mastering risk management, decoding price action, honing a distinctive trading edge, and navigating the intricate realm of the trader's mindset, this invaluable resource provides unparalleled insights to elevate your trading expertise.

www.ingramcontent.com/pod-product-compliance
Lightning Source LLC
Chambersburg PA
CBHW071957210526
45479CB00003B/973